# Kandinsky

PARK
LANE

# The Desire Within

Every revolution has its historical causes and its inner necessity. But there is always one isolated individual, or a group of individuals, who makes the ideas underlying such a revolution their own and puts them into action. European art is rife with great revolutions and true artists, from Giotto and Masaccio, through Leonardo to Caravaggio, to the Impressionists and the Cubists who all, in their own particular way, broke with tradition and developed new approaches to expression.

Vasily Kandinsky was just such an innovator. He broke the last ties that still bound painting to Realism and in so doing he gave a unique impetus to the cultural framework of our time, prompting a major seachange in the way art has developed. His claim was that abstract art would be the art of the future. And no abstract artist ever matched the extraordinary richness of Kandinsky's work. But how did he manage to achieve this new language? By which laws? And how did the change take place?

Kandinksy was over thirty and was a fully-trained lawyer when he left Russia for Germany to become a painter. It is clear, though, that throughout his adolescence and even as far back as his childhood, he was aware of having a certain propensity towards painting. In his autobiography *Rückblicke 1901-1913*, which was published in 1913, he discusses the effects that certain colour harmonies and patterns of lines made on him. Moscow and its crepuscular atmosphere sparked his imagination.

Letting himself go to whatever the future might hold, with his paint box to hand, filled him with enthusiasm for that phenomenon called colour. The young jurist knew the power of the *chiaro-oscuro* practised by Rembrandt and, through the music of Wagner, he discovered the forces that would enable him to transpose impressions into images and colours. He describes his first experience of hearing *Lohengrin* thus, "I saw in my mind's eye all the colours. They were there, in my eyes. Frenetic lines, danced crazily before me."

He was similarly astonished as he gazed on Monet's *Grainstacks*, which he saw at the first-ever exhibition of Impressionist painting, which was held in Moscow in 1895. "Before then," he wrote, "I only knew realist painting, and only the Russians at that [...] And there, all of a sudden, I saw a *painting* [...] There and then I was unable to comprehend that these were actually grainstacks. I had to look it up in the catalogue. The fact that I had not recognized the subject irritated me. I felt that a painter did not have the right to paint in such an obscure fashion. I had a vague feeling that the subject was missing and I was both amazed and annoyed to find that not only did the work exert a powerful suggestion but that it left an unforgettable mark, to the point where all the details, right down to the tiniest, remained somehow in front of your eyes. But all this was very unclear, and I was unable to draw the simple conclusions from it. The only thing that I was sure about was the intensity of the painting, an intensity I would never have imagined to be possible, and which had till then been hidden from me. By means of this intensity, painting was acquiring an amazing strength, an astonishing splendour and, without my noticing it, the subject, as a leading player in the painting, was discredited."

Thoughts such as these were haunting him as he headed for Munich. He was seeking a point of departure for his ideas but the teachings of Anton Azbé or those of the Academy in general did not correspond to what he was seeking. So he painted from models, giving his hand and eye practice. Until 1908, he allowed himself to be influenced by all the contemporary trends, shifting from the traditional academic Naturalism of the Munich school, through to the German Art Nouveau style called Jugendstil, not to mention the other styles he had encountered during his travels. And while, over this period, some of his paintings attracted attention for their sheer mastery of style, others already seemed to be pointing in a new direction.

These were the landscapes where the freshness of the observation came together with rapid draftsmanship. What we see there might be termed "Monumental Impressionism." These are poetic compositions which speak in balletic tones of Mother Russia, romantic villages, medieval knights, as well as Kandinsky's own childhood memories and dreams.

On occasion, the colours on a dark background achieve an intensity which foreshadows the works of his mature years.

Nonetheless, despite their undeniable interest, all these paintings were only a tentative preview of what was to come. Kandinksy's most productive period coincided with his move to Murnau in 1908 and pushed him to explore areas neither he, nor anyone else, had never previously touched upon.

Alternating with his Alpine landscapes, we see paintings with a freer compositional style, with passionate bursts of colour. By now, Kandinsky was acquainted with the work of Cézanne, Gauguin, van Gogh and the other modern masters. He had seen the paintings of Picasso and Matisse, as well as those of the German Expressionists. Popular Russian art, as well as the Bavarian glass-painting tradition, showed him examples of the audacious use of colour.

But at this stage, Kandinsky's experiments were isolated incidents and are insufficient to explain the passion of the early Murnau works, and which are as far from the Fauves as they are from the work of the artists belonging to the Die Brücke school.

In certain paintings, Kandinsky still favoured a relatively structured look. But we often find examples of shapes moving freely in space: we might almost say that they were freely paraphrasing the objects of the real world. His luminous palette is based on the primaries – red, yellow, and blue.

His most frequent subjects, mountains and villages, trees and churches gradually lose their distinguishing features to become pretexts for purely formal and chromatic exercises.

As forms and colour struggle free of each other and become more and more independent, the topic of the painting becomes less imperative. The logical consequence of this trend is for fidelity to nature to be abandoned to the point where there is no connection left with the subject of the painting. Kandinsky himself wrote in his autobiography, "Several years were to go by before I reached the conviction – this more by a process of reasoning than by any sentimental attachment – that nature and art have different organic and historical ends and therefore different means for achieving those ends, but that both are equally valid [...] This conviction was to free me and to give me the key to a new world [...] Everything that was 'dead' began to pulsate with life [...] Everything revealed itself, its very essence, its hidden soul, which was silent more often than not. Thus, each point at rest and each point in movement (which equals the line) came to life and opened up its soul. And this was enough to enable me to seize, with all my being, and with all my senses, the potential and the existence of art, this art which these days, by contrast to what is called the figurative, is termed abstract."

We may trace the artist's progress towards abstraction by looking at his work between 1908 and 1912. Recognizable forms change into formulae, before evolving into completely independent compositions which give free rein to the most diverse associations. Mountains and trees become curving, sinuous lines, animals change into dynamic interactions, people and buildings wind their way into fantastic figures. Meanwhile, colour loses its illustrative function, and representation gives way to composition and improvisation. The title itself is replaced by a number or by a general indication of order. While there are still traces of figuration in the works of 1912 and the years following, the first abstract painting can be dated to 1910, the year in which Kandinsky set out his new aesthetic principles. In his book, *Concerning the Spiritual in Art*, Kandinsky reflected upon the relationship between form and colour, between painting and music. He struggled to define the expressive value of forms and colours and their different combinations. Each colour, he wrote, has its own quality which determines the impression it gives. Yellow is warm, vibrant, and stimulating.

Blue is reposeful, severe, or cold. Red is ardent, passionate, virile. Green is static, neutral, and passive. White conjures up a silence that is pregnant with hidden power, black is a silence with no future.

He also gave forms an interpretation. Yellow is allied to the acute angle and the triangle, while red links up with the right angle, and the square, and blue with the obtuse angle and the circle. Thus optical features are filtered through the observer's emotions to become an elementary means of expression.

"In this fashion," wrote Kandinsky, "each form, and each colour has its own value, what we might call an inner necessity, and this is independent of the reality of exterior objects and reveals itself to the emotions rather than to conceptual research."

In his essay *Point and Line to Plane*, which was published in 1926, Kandinsky attempted to develop a sort of grammar of elementary forms, and their derivatives. Starting from the point, the triangle, the square, and the circle, before moving on to more complex geometric forms, he analyzed the composition of planes from the standpoint of their power to communicate. The point thus becomes a value "in itself", while the line is an element of dynamic tension. According to Kandinsky, the horizontal has a cold powerful force, while the vertical has a hot thrust.

Such a grammar clearly lends itself to endless combinations and permutations and cannot exclude subjective interpretations. Kandinsky was well-aware of this and sought to resolve the problem of finding absolute solutions that might be grasped via the emotions and reason. As he wrote in 1910, "[concepts such as] contrasting tones, unbalance, no longer exist [as] principles [...] opposition and contradictions are our harmony." His early abstract paintings do indeed reveal a deep-rooted inner unease, "Explosions, juxtapositions of splashes of colour, frantic lines, ominous rumblings, catastrophes," were the expression of a convulsive drama which seemed to lack all moderation.

The most varied forms weave their way through space, come into collision while, from the dark depths there emerge strident flashes of light and minuscule whirling particles which disrupt the silence. Everywhere we get the sense that this is a dramatic event, and this is reflected also in the titles of the pieces, which range from the *Deluge* to the *Last Judgment*.

No sooner do we manage to make out a shape, than it disappears once again into the depths. The multiplicity of forms and the power of the movement come together in the most extreme forms, and yet the outcome is never chaotic. Studied correspondences, cesurae, force fields, and stresses, attest to the presence of a vibrant order with an inner tension, and this is what makes these pieces exceptional, unique.

"When you create a work of art, you create a world," wrote Kandinsky. For him, art was always an adventure into the fantastical for, in the restricted universe of the painting, the observer must be able to sense the primary forces of creation at work.

"Art," he added, "cannot be great unless it is in direct contact with the cosmic forces, and if it allows itself to be governed by them. These laws can be felt, almost unconsciously, when we come into contact with nature, not just on the outside but deep down. One should not stop at looking, one must experience."

The richest and the most exuberant painting techniques must submit to these limits. Kandinsky's initial violent response to his liberation from the subject was followed by a period of meditation and clarification. "At the start of 1914," wrote the artist, "I felt the need for a cool tranquillity. I did not want rigidity, but coldness, a great coldness. And oftentimes, ice [...] something burning hot within a container made of ice."

This new phase of the artist's development blossomed during his period as a lecturer at the Weimar Bauhaus. The structure of his paintings became stricter while the geometric shapes shifted into a more irregular mode. From that time on, ruler and compasses became an integral part of the artist's wherewithal. Curves and straight lines seem to be set out in a systematic, yet highly-poetic, fashion.

Colour and form are strongly linked, with the surface of the canvas taking the role of an active background. While some of the canvases of this period seem to illustrate the ideas postulated in *Point and Line to Plane*, these geometric works, are very much more than the expression of a theory "in paint" of a purely intellectual experience.

"The head," wrote the artist, "is a necessary and important part of the human body but only if it has established an organic relationship with the heart and the emotions [...] Without such a relationship, the head is the source of all manner of dangers and distortions. This is true in all areas and no less so in art."

It is in fact from the emotional point of view that these pure, perfectly-wrought forms and carefully measured-out colours come into their own. What they are doing is revealing the "burning hot content" within the "ice-cold container." Tension and relaxation, rhythm and latent movement imbue these geometric constructions with a fantastical input, and in so doing betray their connection with the paintings of Kandinsky's earlier period.

In the meantime, the signs of a new approach were emerging. Kandinsky's interpretation of geometric forms evolved into ever-more magical and spiritual directions. We see plant and animal shapes taking over from the geometric, while the sombre and flat colours become infused with a new intensity. There is an almost romantic feel to Kandinsky's works of the period 1926-1929, this both in the modern, as well as in the more traditional, sense of the word.

We can retrace many of the themes examined in earlier times when we look at the paintings of Kandinsky's Paris period, but they have undergone a strange transformation.

The geometric figures, the tectonic divisions, and the regular forms come together with ornamental signs which suggest hieroglyphs or elementary organic symbols. The surface of the painting suggests an irrational space, while the interaction between the figures is played out with a lighter than air sweep of elegant arabesque-like curves.

A brilliant and exotic palette highlights the inspired invention of these shapes which, however far they might be from nature, still maintain their heritage and can be said to celebrate a natural world that is out-of-the-ordinary.

In a word, Kandinsky's tireless faith in the inexhaustible wealth of expression of form and colour – independently of its physical reality – is, we might almost say, proclaimed in the works he executed in Paris.

It is not easy to judge Kandinsky's work overall. Not only was his range too great, but his period of operation was too long, and his career, which extended from landscape sketches and culminated with his paintings in Paris, was too varied.

In looking at the work of Kandinsky, not only do we see a person whose power to create seems boundless, and who was capable of embracing limitless variations of style, but we also bear witness to one of the most extraordinary aesthetic revolutions ever to take place. Intuition and reflection, imagination and reason, passion and restraint, a Slav soul and a western spirit all contributed to shaping the man and the artist.

An indefatigable promoter of abstract art, Vasily Kandinsky believed nonetheless in the unity of all forms of art and in the grace that had been accorded him to be involved. As he wrote, "Art remains silent to those who do not wish to listen to form. Yes indeed, and this is not the case of abstract art but all forms of art, including the most realistic."

Vasily Kandinsky was born in Moscow on 4 December 1866. When he was about five years old, the family moved to Odessa, where he went to school. In 1886 he moved back to Moscow to study law and economics at university. After graduation, he became an assistant in the university's Law faculty.

Kandinsky visited Paris in 1889 and 1892. He saw the extensive exhibition of the work of the French Impressionists in Moscow in 1895 and saw the art collection at the Hermitage in Leningrad four years later. These experiences helped fire his enthusiasm for painting and, when he was offered a chair in the University of Dorpat in Esthonia in 1896, he decided to change course once and for all.

Moving to Munich with his cousin Anya Tichceva who had become his wife some years earlier, he set about studying art. At that time, Munich was in the forefront of the Art Nouveau movement and Kandinsky trained initially under Anton Azbé before moving on to the Academy where Franz Stuck was his teacher.

In 1901, Kandinsky set up the Phalanx group. In the following year, he met the painter Gabriele Münter, with whom he set up home and with whom he travelled extensively over the next thirteen years.

Between June 1906 and June 1907, Kandinsky lived in Sèvres, just outside Paris. Awarded a Grand Prix at the Salon d'Automne, he nonetheless eschewed the most modern tendencies. In 1908, he returned to Munich before moving to Murnau. His landscapes of the latter area, as well as his first *Improvisations* were executed in 1909, which was the same year in which the Neue Künstler Vereinigung (New Artists Federation) was established, with Kandinsky as president. His first abstract watercolour dates from the following year, as do his first three *Compositions* and the first draft of his treatise *Concerning the Spiritual in Art.*

This was a very important period for Kandinsky, particularly in terms of the people with whom he came into contact. In 1908, he met Alexis Jawlensky and Marianne von Werefkin. Two years later, he made the acquaintance of Franz Marc, in 1911 Paul Klee, Hans Arp, and August Macke. In that same year, he established the Blaue Reiter (The Blue Rider) group with Franz Marc. Others in the group included Klee, Macke, Alfred Kubin, Heinrich Campendonk, and Gabrielle Münter. The group exhibited first in Munich and then, a short time later, at the Sturm Gallery in Berlin. The advent of the First World War put paid to Der Blaue Reiter's activities and it was dissolved after one last show in Berlin.

Kandinsky made his way back to Moscow and, having left Gabriele Münter in 1916 for the last time, in the following February, married a fellow Russian, Nina von Andreevsky, with whom he stayed until his death.

As a result of the October Revolution, Kandinsky was appointed to membership of the Department of Fine Arts in the People's Committee for Public Education. He also gained a teaching post in the state art workshops. In 1919, he established the Museum of Painting Culture. One year later, he was nominated to a lectureship in the University of Moscow where, within a year he had founded the Academy for the Artistic Sciences, and was elected its Vice-President. Later that same year, he moved to Berlin. In 1922, he took up a lectureship at the Weimar Bauhaus. In 1924, he joined Klee, Feininger, and Jawlensky in setting up Der Blaue Vier group. That same year travel became a major feature of his life, and he visited Austria, Switzerland, Italy, and France, getting as far afield as Palestine, Syria, Turkey, and Greece. One year later, the Bauhaus moved to Dessau and Kandinsky moved with it. He published *Point and Line to Plane* in Munich in 1926. Meanwhile, his teaching and painting were starting to attract considerable critical acclaim and he exhibited widely, including twice in Paris, in 1929 and 1930.

In 1933, the Nazis shut down the Bauhaus and Kandinsky, who had obtained German nationality in 1928, headed for Paris. Meanwhile, in Germany, the paintings he had left behind were seized and sold off to the lowest bidder. Having obtained French nationality at the outbreak of the Second World War, Kandinsky continued to work hard, the Occupation not stemming his output. Vasily Kandinsky died in Paris on 13 December 1944 at the age of 78.

1. Der Blaue Reiter (The Blue Rider) – 1903. Bührle Collection, Zurich – *This well-known painting dates from the period Kandinsky spent in Munich seeking new ways of using images and colour. Through the agency of the Blaue Reiter group, Kandinsky achieved the departure points he was seeking: to distil the creative spark for his paintings from the forces of nature and instinct. The romantic image of the rider and his white horse galloping on the hillside symbolizes energy and dynamism.*

2. Russian Belle and Landscape – 1905. Städtische Galerie, Munich – *This canvas, with its romantic elements, belongs to Kandinsky's youth. "At that time" wrote the artist, "I was seeking to express the musicality of the Russian landscape by using strong outlines and small specks of colour."*

3. The Murnau Road – 1909. Private collection – *The multi-coloured roofs of Murnau and the bright yellow of the walls animate this painting of 1909. This view, which was very precious to the artist and which he painted many times, reveals his naturalist vision during this exploratory period, and offers an analysis of rhythm, a study of colours, and a tendency towards abstraction.*

4. Arab Cemetery – 1909. Kunsthalle, Hamburg – *This is another canvas from the early years of the century. Kandinsky was working on a new conception of the painted image during this period and here he uses strong lines, as well as powerful, clear colours with some particularly lovely shades of red, blue, and orange. While tending towards abstraction, the forms and figures, which are outlined in black, are nonetheless very realistic.*

5. Railroad near Murnau – 1909. Städtische Galerie im Lenbachhaus, Munich – *As in the case of all his other work during this period, this work shows Kandinsky's gradual shift into abstract art. The houses and the trees are now but lines. The colours seem to strive to break loose from their illustrative role towards the improvisational. The movement is conveyed by the black train which cuts across the multi-hued landscape.*

6. Improvisation VIII – 1909. Private collection – *This vague and generic title was used for a number of paintings executed in the early years of the century. At that time, Kandinsky was striving to approach art with as much freedom as possible and he achieved this by getting more and more abstract to the point that many of his paintings look as if they were created spontaneously and draw from no particular cultural background. This* Improvisation *is noteworthy for its power and the luminous quality of the colours.*

7. Landscape with Tower – 1909. Musée National d'Art Moderne, Centre Georges Pompidou, Paris – *In this landscape, which was executed during Kandinsky's Murnau period, the colours are more violent and nature is informed with a new energy while the fidelity to the way things look takes a lesser role. The painter's ultimate aim was to transform the subject into one element of the composition.*

8. Paradise – 1909. Private collection – *Rather than each detail having its own significance, the way they are put together is what counts, the harmony of the whole, the abundance of the ornamentation, the power of expression inherent in the colours, although the topics are still in the same shades as they have in nature.*

9. Improvisation VI – 1909. Städtische Galerie, Munich – *This painting has no specific title. As in the case of the others in this series, its vitality comes from the elementary forms created by colour and line. We still see some silhouettes of people, houses, and trees but they do not have a precise significance.*

10. The Cow – 1910. Städtische Galerie im Lenbachhaus, Munich – *In this oil on canvas of 1910 the patches of colour express themselves freely to create an abstract vision. The hill is represented by the wide arc of the irregular blue and yellow circle while the white cow dominates the foreground. The artist seemed to enjoy recreating nature but he wished it to be incomprehensible and abstract.*

11. First Abstract Watercolour – 1910. Musée National d'Art Moderne, Centre Georges Pompidou, Paris – *The importance of this painting is that it is the first of the non-figurative period in painting. A number of critics have suggested that the artist was intending to recreate the first contact a person might have with an unknown world. The result is a collection of lines, colours, and shapes, which show unidentifiable objects and create a magnificent* graffito *effect.*

12. Improvisation XVIII – 1911. Städtische Galerie im Lenbachhaus, Munich – *The topic of this painting was reprised in the following year. Each of the paintings with this title have their own significance and this one is important for the fact that it marks a stage in Kandinsky's shift from figurative to abstract art.*

13. Composition IV – 1911. Kunstsammlung Nordrhein-Westfalen, Düsseldorf – *The thick black lines mixing with the bright colours and the stylized forms enable the artist to create a new language whose form and meaning changed constantly. For the painter, art was becoming an aesthetic operation.*

14. Improvisation V (Park) – 1911. Musée National d'Art Moderne, Centre Georges Pompidou, Paris – *Bursting with colours, this 1911 canvas is cross-cut with black lines which are used in an attempt to define the abstract forms of the original. As with all his paintings of the period, Kandinsky gives the impression of having painted in a totally unrestrained, spontaneous way.*

15. Horseman – 1911. Städtische Galerie im Lenbachhaus, Munich – *Kandinsky's work at the start of the century seemed to break free from all the conceptions of traditional art. As a result, the observer's eye is caught by a number of new stimuli and he or she is led to see the work as a purely aesthetic creation. This* Horseman *belongs to the period when the artist was a member of the Blaue Reiter group.*

16. Sketch for the *"Blaue Reiter Almanach"* (Blue Rider Almanac) – 1911. Städtische Galerie im Lenbachhaus, Munich – *This sketch was produced for inclusion in the Almanach of the Blaue Reiter group, a publication designed to disseminate the theories of this new movement of which Kandinsky was one of the most vigourous supporters. The rider and his horse are clearly the work of a master, the clear-cut lines and well-defined contours enhance the upward movement of the figure.*

17. St George – 1911. Städtische Galerie im Lenbachhaus, Munich – *Kandinsky was long fascinated by the theme of the horse and rider and addressed the topic many times. In this painting, which shows St George battling the dragon, the movement and the energy of the figures as they force their way upwards reveal that the aim of the picture is to stress the feeling of power rather than to transmit forms.*

18. Sketch for the *"Blaue Reiter Almanach"* (Blue Rider Almanac) – 1911. Städtische Galerie im Lenbachhaus, Munich – *Another horse and rider in this 1911 picture. This romantic figure was a common feature of the work of Kandinsky throughout his years of involvement with the Blaue Reiter group, and was, for the artist, not only a talisman, but also the hero of his dreams, and a symbol of the cosmic forces.*

19. Sketch for the *"Blaue Reiter Almanach"* (Blue Rider Almanac) – 1911. Städtische Galerie im Lenbachhaus, Munich – *Once again the horse and rider strive upwards in a powerful surge of movement. This sketch was published in the Almanach that Kandinsky had established in collaboration with his friend the painter Franz Marc and other artists who shared the same convictions regarding the new theories of art which posited the idea of breaking free from all restrictions.*

20. All Saints – 1911. Städtische Galerie im Lenbachhaus, Munich – *The summer of 1911 was an extremely important period for the career of Kandinsky. He was living in Murnau at the time and had just started editing the Almanach which was published in the following year. In his painting, he was moving further and further from the figurative and towards the completely abstract, as can be seen from this remarkable canvas which has a religious theme.*

21. Improvisation XXVI – 1912. Städtische Galerie, Munich – *In this painting, objective reality has finally disappeared although this does not exclude the possibility of one's being able to make associations. The principle of the independence of form and colour from the world of things is affirmed in full in this "improvisation".*

22. Avec l'Arc Noir – 1912. Musée National d'Art Moderne, Centre Georges Pompidou, Paris – *Variously-coloured and shaped lines and planes come together in a strikingly violent composition. Kandinsky's works in this period are shot through with a cosmic thrill. "Creating a work of art means creating a world", wrote the artist.*

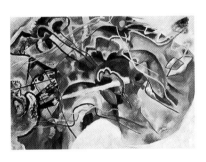

23. Painting with a White Border – 1913. The Solomon R. Guggenheim Museum, New York – *It is probable that this piece was inspired by a visit by the artist to Russia. We see a troika on the left-hand side of the canvas while, in the centre, the horseman, who is more than likely Saint George, and who is armed with a long white lance, confronts the dragon. There are also a number of other images which, from the preparatory sketches onwards, have gradually become abstract forms.*

24. Black Lines – 1913. The Solomon R. Guggenheim Museum, New York – *The bright colours and the perfect balance of forms make this oil on canvas a truly exceptional moment in Kandinsky's career. While it is not very easy to decipher what he intended, it is as well to bear in mind what the artist himself wrote: "the content is merely what the observer can perceive under the effect of the colours and shapes." It is undeniable that such a magnificent explosion of colour has an extraordinary impact on the viewer.*

25. Red and Blue – 1913. Private collection – *Once again we have a painting whose title evokes colours. The symbolism of colour was much in vogue in literary and painting circles at the time and, in his* Concerning the Spiritual in Art *Kandinsky wrote about the colour blue: "The deeper it gets the more one is drawn towards the infinite." Here we see the patches of blue, in many shades, softening the intensity of the red, the orange, and the yellow.*

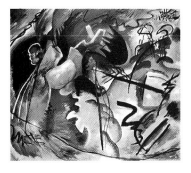

26. Painting with White Shapes – 1913. The Solomon R. Guggenheim Museum, New York – *This painting belongs to what is commonly referred to as Kandinsky's Blue Rider period when the artist and his friends were first showing in Munich and provoking considerable controversy with what were regarded as very strange ideas indeed. Kandinsky was one of the most pilloried as well as being one of the most admired, and soon became the leader. Looking at this picture we can quite appreciate the astonishment and interest that their work was arousing.*

27. Painting with Red Splash – 1914. Musée National d'Art Moderne, Centre Georges Pompidou, Paris – *The patches of bright colour from Kandinsky's palette offer themselves up in all their beauty to the observer who feels drawn into the work. The splashes of red mix with those of other colours to create an extraordinary* graffito *effect.*

28. Improvisation XXXV – 1914. Kunstmuseum, Basel – *The juxtaposition of such diverse objects creates an extremely dramatic effect. While giving a feeling of movement, the diagonals also act as stabilizers.*

29. Untitled, Known as "Deluge" – 1914. Städtische Galerie, Munich – *The dramatic power of Kandinsky's vision reaches its peak in paintings such as this. Uncontrolled forces break loose, a whirlwind effect overwhelms the space and all human dimension is lost. A boundless catastrophe is unleashed.*

30. Untitled Improvisation – 1914. Städtische Galerie, Munich – *The shock and the whirling of diverse shapes, all criteria of order seem to have been lost. And yet the distribution of the colours, the power of the vast curve, and the relationships between the different components ensure that total confusion is avoided.*

31. The Horseman of the Apocalypse – 1914. Städtische Galerie in Lenbachhaus, Munich – *Captivated by Bavarian popular art which he had seen at Murnau, and enthused by the idea of illustrating the Bible with a number of friends, Kandinsky painted this religiously-inspired scene in 1914. He was undoubtedly inspired by a sentence written by his friend Franz Marc two years earlier: "In the face of innovative works one feels as if one is dreaming and one can hear the Four Horsemen of the Apocalypse".*

32. Painting with Three Splashes – 1914. The Solomon R. Guggenheim Museum, New York – *The range of colours is the special feature of this painting too. The seemingly-endless tones of red, orange, green, and purplish-blue can be seen all over the canvas and alternate to form a concentric ribbon of colour. The painting looks like a astonishing palette with the three main patches of colour standing out.*

33. Black Splash – 1921. Kunsthaus, Zurich – *In his first treatise, which was entitled* Concerning the Spiritual in Art, *Kandinsky declared that each shape and colour has its own characteristic, which is not objective but which acts as a psychological stimulus. As far as the artist is concerned, colours are reinforced by shapes. In this painting, the forms and colours seem to float against the background, like a game.*

34. In the Black Square – 1923. The Solomon R. Guggenheim Museum, New York – *When, in about 1920, he moved on to exploring the world of pure forms and individual colours, Kandinsky was breaking quite dramatically with his previous work. Geometrical shapes became his instruments.*

35. Contact – 1924. Galerie Maeght, Paris – *Kandinsky produced this painting after he had been at the Weimar Bauhaus for two years, where he had been lecturing and taking part in the experiments for which the school made its name. In his teaching, Kandinsky laid stress on colour and forms in space, from the most simple shapes such as the triangle, the line and the circle. This canvas represents his theories: the triangles, the lines and circles evolve in total freedom.*

36. Composition – 1924. Private collection – *This is another painting from Kandinsky's sojourn at the Bauhaus and is typical of what the critics have dubbed his "Cold period". At this time, the artist referred to this stage in his career as the time when "means of expression were being stripped bare." In this* Composition, *the colours are reassuring and the forms move freely as if they were floating in the heart of the cosmos.*

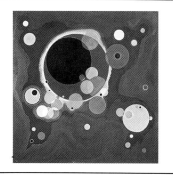

37. Several Circles – 1926. The Solomon R. Guggenheim Museum, New York – *The theories of the Bauhaus group gave priority to the circle as "the symbol of eternity and the infinite" whose fundamental colours were red, blue, yellow, and purple. Kandinsky wrote to a critic thus, "you have commented on my predilection for the circle. This simple, essential, and versatile form fascinates me for it offers infinite possibilities."*

38. Tranchant dans la douceur – 1929. Galerie Maeght, Paris – *A greyish background, with geometric forms and sombre colours are the salient features of this painting with its astonishing title. This is another example of the sensitivity that led the Bauhaus artists to believe that colours could be hot or cold, dynamic or passive, violent or peaceable, and could have a positive or negative effect on the observer.*

39. Yellow, Red, Blue – 1925. Musée National d'Art Moderne, Centre Georges Pompidou, Paris – *Regular shapes such as circles and rectangles are mixed in with free-flowing, imaginative traits such as the serpentine black line. The relevance of the painting resides in the dialectic between the two types of forms.*

40. Points – 1934. Private collection – *Kandinsky loved testing out theories to their extremes, as can be seen in this painting which grew out of one of his experiments with the point and the line. The artist liked to remark, not without humour, that the point could be made with a sharp implement while a paintbrush loaded with colour was needed to make the mark.*

41. Black Points – 1937. Private collection – *Taking as his cue the idea that the point is the most concise form, Kandinsky experimented it widely. In this painting, which dates from 1937, the artist took pleasure in putting into practice the concept that, in the world of art, the point uses its own power to develop in the particular way it wishes.*

42. Voltige – 1935. The Solomon R. Guggenheim Museum, New York – *An evocative title for this splendid canvas where forms and space are treated lightly. A wide range of colours take part in this "flying trapeze act". Red ("an essentially warm and boundless colour"), purple ("a chilled red"), black ("nothingness"), and blue which was Kandinsky's favourite.*

43. Movement I – 1935. Private collection – *Compared to the dramatic compositions that he painted between 1912 and 1914, this* Mouvement I *seems startlingly calm and well-balanced. We are transported into an extraordinary sky, which is peopled with fabulous, gently-swirling images.*

44. Sky Blue – 1940. Musée National d'Art Moderne, Centre Georges Pompidou, Paris – *The sky is very light and the floating figures remind one of micro-organisms. And yet they have no connection with the plant or animal world. They are the fruits of the artist's imagination and are set against a space that is no less fantastical and unreal.*

45. Tempered Élan – 1944. Musée National d'Art Moderne, Centre Georges Pompidou, Paris – *There is a strange melancholy feel to this painting, which was the artist's last completed canvas. The purple in the background tones in with the reds, blues, greens, and browns of the fanciful images, the largest of which stretches across the entire picture.*

1. *Der Blaue Reiter* (The Blue Rider) – 1903. Bührle Collection, Zurich.

2. *Russian Belle and Landscape* – 1905.
   Städtische Galerie, Munich.

3. *The Murnau Road* – 1909. Private collection.

4. *Arab Cemetery* – 1909. Kunsthalle, Hamburg.

5. *Railroad near Murnau* – 1909.
Städtische Galerie im Lenbachhaus, Munich.

7. *Landscape with Tower* – 1909. Musée National d'Art Moderne, Centre Georges Pompidou, Paris.

6. *Improvisation VIII* – 1909.
   Private collection.

8. *Paradise* – 1909. Private collection.

9. *Improvisation VI* – 1909.
Städtische Galerie, Munich.

10.  *The Cow* – 1910. Städtische Galerie im Lenbachhaus, Munich.

11. *First Abstract Watercolour* – 1910. Musée National d'Art Moderne,
Centre Georges Pompidou, Paris.

12. *Improvisation XVIII* – 1911. Städtische Galerie im Lenbachhaus, Munich.

13. *Composition IV* – 1911. Kunstsammlung Nordrhein-Westfalen, Düsseldorf.

14. *Improvisation V (Park)* – 1911. Musée National d'Art Moderne,
Centre Georges Pompidou, Paris.

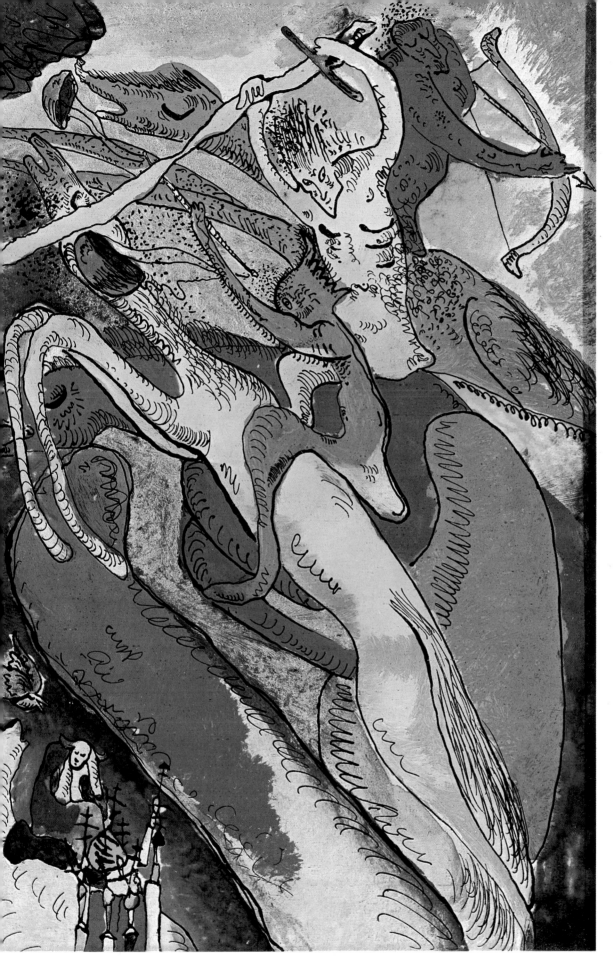

15. *Horseman* – 1911. Städtische Galerie im Lenbachhaus, Munich.

16. *Sketch for the* "Blaue Reiter Almanach" *(Blue Rider Almanac)* – 1911. Städtische Galerie im Lenbachhaus, Munich.

17. *St George* – 1911.
Städtische Galerie
im Lenbachhaus, Munich.

18. *Sketch for the* "Blaue Reiter Almanach" *(Blue Rider Almanac)* – 1911.
    Städtische Galerie im Lenbachhaus, Munich.

19. *Sketch for the* "Blaue Reiter Almanach" *(Blue Rider Almanac)* – 1911.
Städtische Galerie im Lenbachhaus, Munich.

20. *All Saints* – 1911. Städtische Galerie im Lenbachhaus, Munich.

21. *Improvisation XXVI* – 1912. Städtische Galerie, Munich.

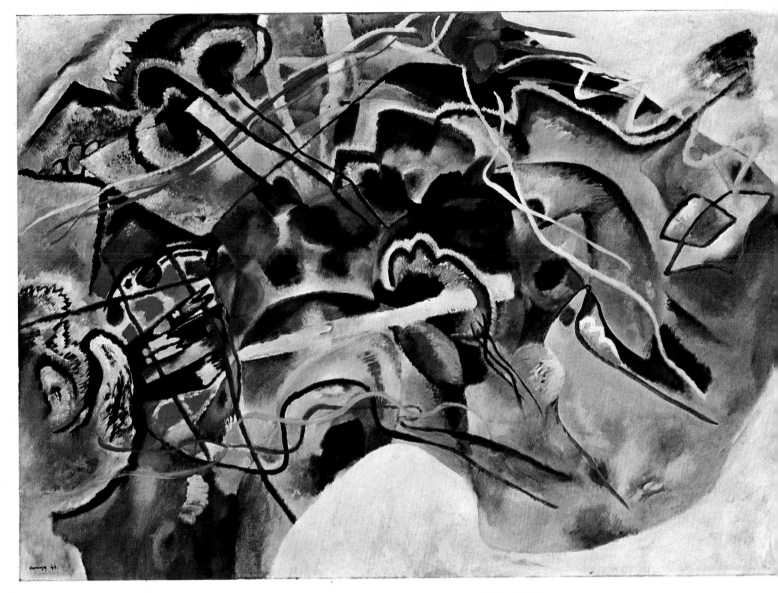

23. *Painting with a White Border* – 1913. The Solomon R. Guggenheim Museum, New York.

22. *Avec l'Arc Noir* – 1912.
    Musée National d'Art Moderne, Centre Georges Pompidou, Paris.

24. *Black Lines* – 1913. The Solomon R. Guggenheim Museum, New York.

25. *Red and Blue* – 1913. Private collection.

26. *Painting with White Shapes* – 1913. The Solomon R. Guggenheim Museum, New York.

27. *Painting with Red Splash* – 1914.
    Musée National d'Art Moderne, Centre Georges Pompidou, Paris.

28. *Improvisation XXXV* – 1914. Kunstmuseum, Basel.

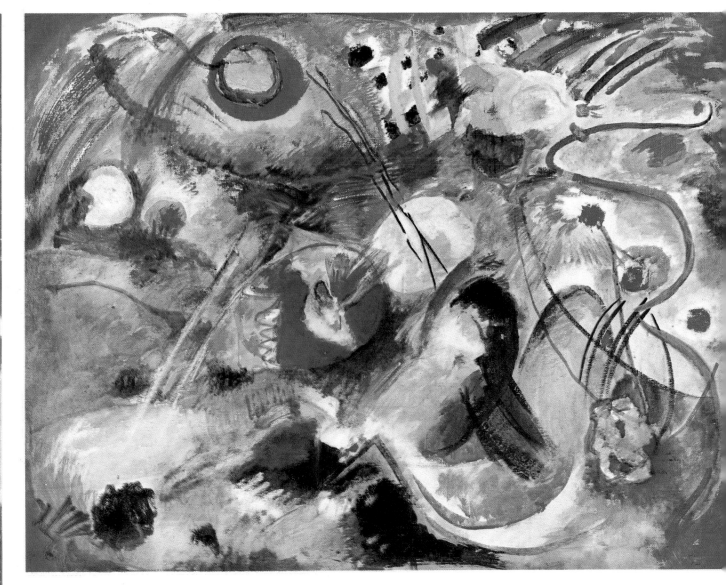

29. *Untitled, Known as "Deluge"* – 1914. Städtische Galerie, Munich.

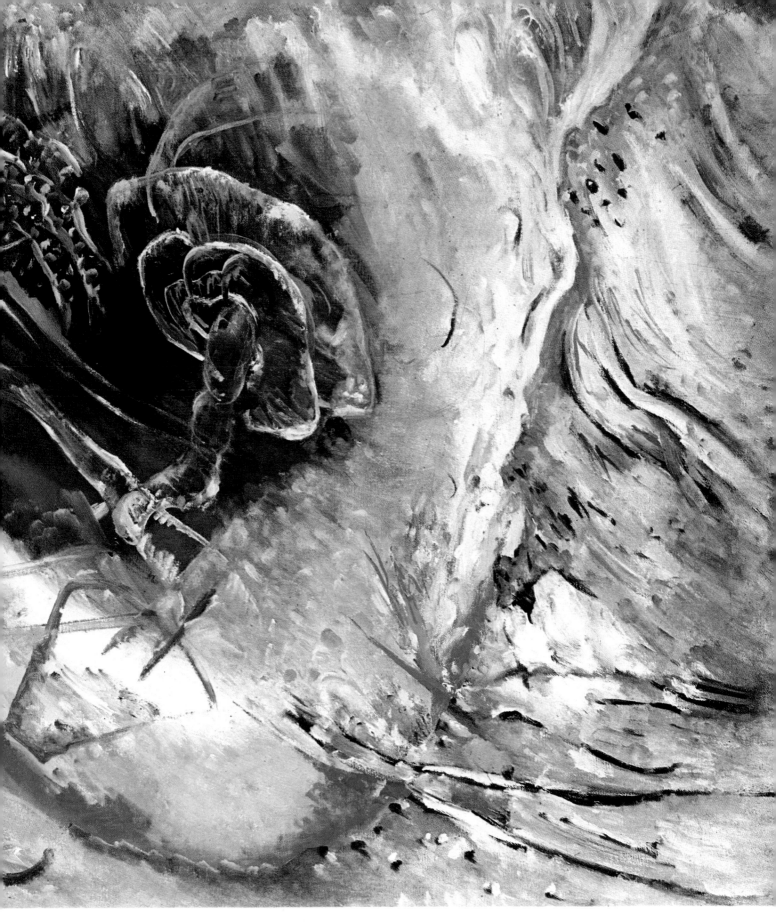

30. *Untitled*
*Improvisation –*
1914.
Städtische Galerie,
Munich.

31. *The Horseman of the Apocalypse* – 1914.
    Städtische Galerie in Lenbachhaus, Munich.

32. *Painting with Three Splashes* – 1914. The Solomon R. Guggenheim Museum, New York.

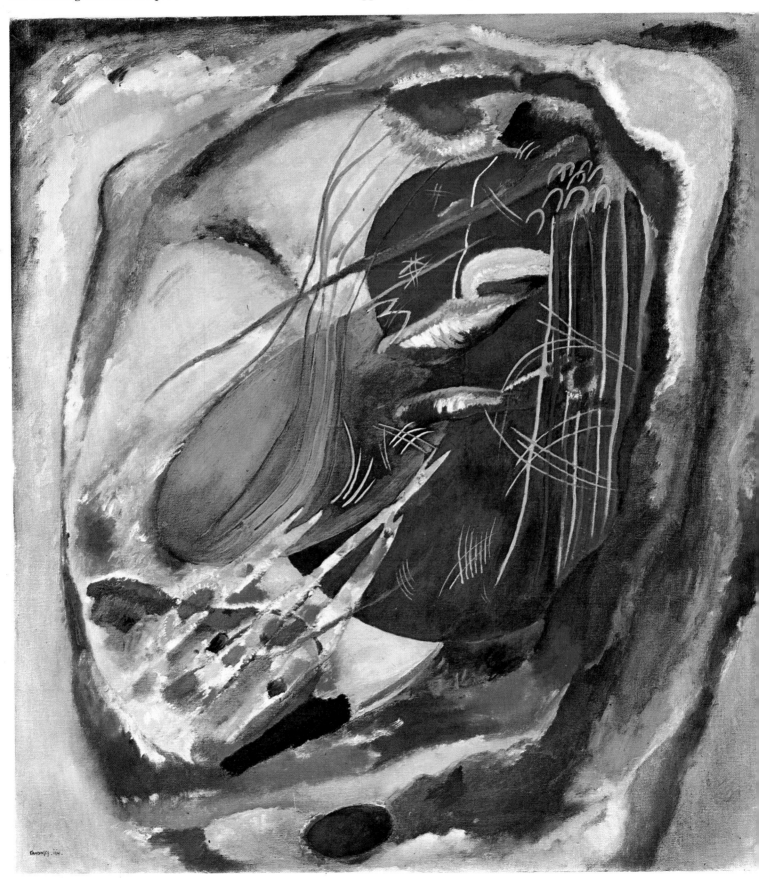

33. *Black Splash* – 1921. Kunsthaus, Zurich.

34. *In the Black Square* – 1923. The Solomon R. Guggenheim Museum, New York.

35. *Contact* – 1924.
Galerie Maeght, Paris.

36. *Composition* – 1924.
Private collection.

37. *Several Circles* – 1926. The Solomon R. Guggenheim Museum, New York.

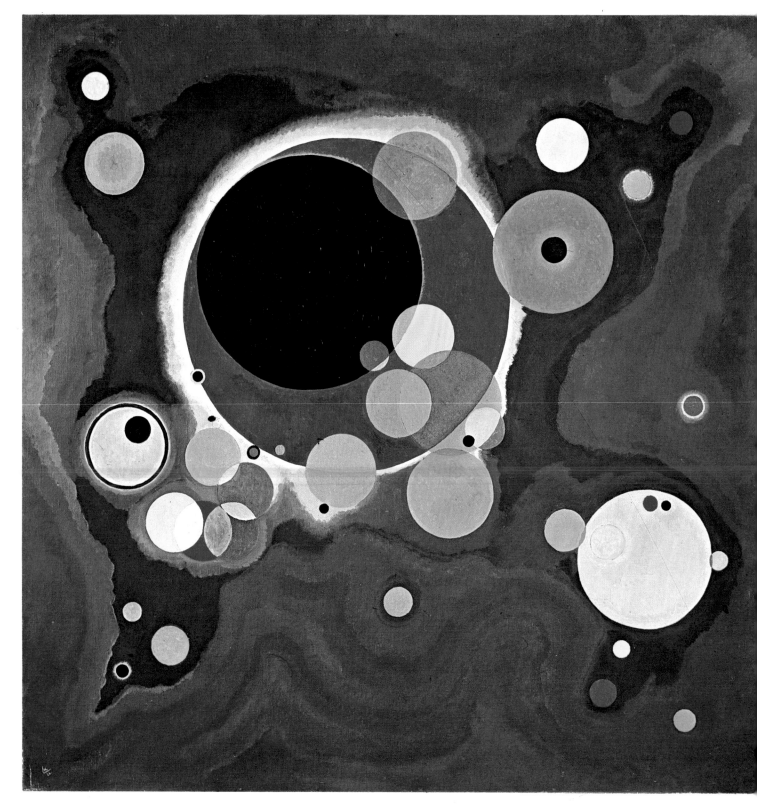

38.  *Tranchant dans la douceur* – 1929. Galerie Maeght, Paris.

39.  *Yellow, Red, Blue* – 1925.
Musée National d'Art Moderne,
Centre Georges Pompidou, Paris.

40. *Points* – 1934. Private collection.

41. *Black Points* – 1937. Private collection.

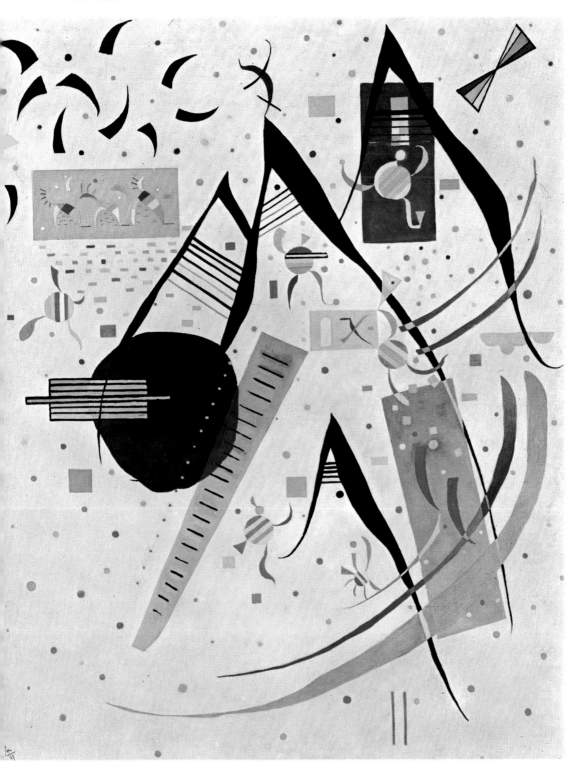

42. *Voltige* – 1935. The Solomon R. Guggenheim Museum, New York.

43. *Movement I* – 1935.
Private collection.

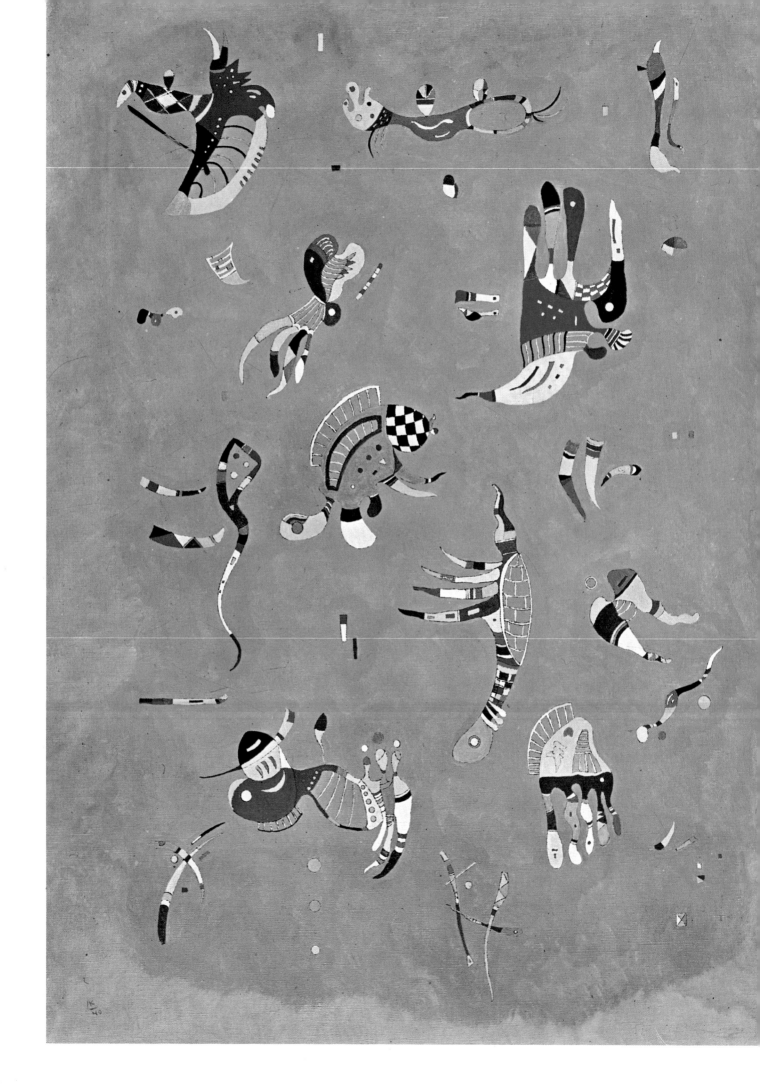

44. *Sky Blue* – 1940.
    Musée National d'Art Moderne,
    Centre Georges Pompidou, Paris.

45. *Tempered Élan* – 1944. Musée National d'Art Moderne,
    Centre Georges Pompidou, Paris.

*Editor in chief* Anna Maria Mascheroni

*Art director* Luciano Raimondi

*Text* Peter Anselm Riedl

*Translation* Roberta Kedzieski

*Production* Art, Bologna

*Photo credits* Gruppo Editoriale Fabbri S.p.A., Milan

Text and illustrations are taken from the series "Maestri del Colore"
© 1963 Fabbri Editori, Milan

Copyright © 1992 by Gruppo Editoriale Fabbri S.p.A., Milan

© S.I.A.E. 1993, Rome, for the works by Vasily Kandinsky

Published by Park Lane
An Imprint of Grange Books Ltd
The Grange
Grange Yard
LONDON
SE1 3AG

ISBN 1-85627-249-4

This edition published 1993

Printed in Italy by Gruppo Editoriale Fabbri S.p.A., Milan

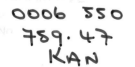